EARTH FIGURED OUT

Earth's Landforms

Nancy Dickmann

Cavendish Square

New York

Published in 2016 by Cavendish Square Publishing, LLC
243 5th Avenue, Suite 136, New York, NY 10016

Website: cavendishsq.com

This publication represents the opinions and views of the author based on his or her personal
experience, knowledge, and research. The information in this book serves as a general guide only.
The author and publisher have used their best efforts in preparing this book and disclaim liability
rising directly or indirectly from the use and application of this book.

CPSIA Compliance Information: Batch #CW16CSQ

All websites were available and accurate when this book was sent to press.

Cataloging-in-Publication Data

Dickmann, Nancy.
Earth's landforms / by Nancy Dickmann.
p. cm. — (Earth figured out)
Includes index.
ISBN 978-1-5026-0868-0 (hardcover) ISBN 978-1-5026-0866-6 (paperback)
ISBN 978-1-5026-0869-7 (e-book)
1. Landforms — Juvenile literature. I. Dickmann, Nancy. II. Title.
GB406.D53 2016
551.41—d23

Produced for Cavendish Square by Calcium
Editors: Sarah Eason and Harriet McGregor
Designer: Paul Myerscough

Picture credits: Cover Francesco R. Iacomino/Shutterstock; Insides: NASA: 11; Shutterstock:
Marcos Amend 18, Thomas Barrat 14–15, Canadastock 6, ChrisVanLennepPhoto 17, Budkov
Denis 9, Asaf Eliason 16, Marisa Estivill 20–21, Ammit Jack 8–9, Kavram 10, Andrzej Kubik 29,
Doug Meek 26, R McIntyre 24–25, Alice Nerr 22–23, Mati Nitibhon 15, Pecold 22, Vadim Petrakov
18-19, Ralwel 4–5, Santi Rodriguez 26–27, Nicram Sabod 5, Susan Schmitz 1, 21, Konstantin
Stepanenko 25, Szefei 28–29, Jolanta Wojcicka 12–13, YuG 6–7; Wikimedia Commons: 13.

Printed in the United States of America

Contents

Our Amazing Planet

Our home planet, Earth, is an amazing place. The land is covered with tall mountains and steep **cliffs**, winding rivers and calm lakes. It also has dry **deserts**, **fertile prairies**, and lush **rain forests**. Even beneath the ground, cave systems stretch for miles. The oceans are also full of life, and deep beneath the water's surface are features that look like those on the land: trenches, mountains, and even **volcanoes**.

All of these amazing features are landforms, and they provide a wide range of **habitats** for Earth's many plants and animals. Landforms may seem permanent, but they are constantly changing, as new ones form and old ones disappear. When Earth was first formed, it looked very different. Millions of years of moving rock and water have shaped the planet into what we know today.

EARTH FIGURED OUT

Landforms are not only found on Earth. For example, the moon has mountains, valleys, and plains. The rocky planets Venus and Mars are dotted with volcanoes. Mars is home to a huge system of **canyons**, the Valles Marineris. It is almost as long as the United States is wide, and four times as deep as the Grand Canyon!

Beautiful oceans of liquid water cover more than two-thirds of Earth's surface.

Amazing **fjords**, like this one in Norway, are formed by icy **glaciers** carving out the landscape.

Mountains and Valleys

Mountains are some of the most impressive landforms on Earth. Their towering peaks seem to stretch toward the sky. Many are so high that they are always covered with ice and snow. Earth's highest mountain, Mount Everest, is an amazing 29,035 feet (8,850 meters) tall. That's almost eleven times higher than the world's tallest building!

Earth's **crust** is made up of many smaller pieces called **tectonic plates**. These plates "float" on top of the softer **molten** rock inside Earth, like pieces of an eggshell. The plates are constantly moving around, and when two plates push up against each other, mountains can form. The pressure of the two plates forces rock upward in a process that can take millions of years. The uplifted rock forms a mountain range, with many individual peaks.

Many mountain valleys form an important habitat for plants and animals, which are specially adapted to live there.

The Himalayas are the world's highest mountain range. They formed when the land that is now India collided with the rest of Asia. They are still growing.

EARTH FIGURED OUT

Between mountains or hills, you'll find valleys. These long, thin areas of lower ground can be formed in different ways. Some were carved out by the movement of huge glaciers.

Others were formed when a river made its way through, grinding down the rock and soil and then carrying it away. Many early humans settled in valleys.

Volcanoes

One type of mountain is a little more unpredictable than the others: volcanoes. These mountains can sometimes **erupt**, spewing out ash, gases, and molten rock called **lava**. The lava eventually hardens to form new rock.

Some volcanoes form where two tectonic plates are moving away from each other, leaving a gap in the Earth's crust. **Magma** rises from beneath to fill the gap. Other types of volcanoes are formed when two plates are pushed together. One of the plates is forced beneath the other one, forming a subduction zone. The sinking plate heats up and releases water, which helps melt the rock. When this magma reaches the surface, volcanoes are formed.

A few volcanoes form over places called "hot spots." These are places where there is a large area of unusually hot rock beneath the surface. Hot spots beneath the oceans can form volcanic islands. The islands of Hawaii were formed in this way.

EARTH FIGURED OUT

When volcanoes erupt, they spew out molten rock called lava. Eruptions underneath water or ice make a type of lava called pillow lava. Above ground, lava that cools slowly, without moving too fast, will form pahoehoe. A type of lava called a'a cools more quickly while it is moving fast, forming a rough, jagged surface.

It is hard to tell when
a volcano will erupt.
Some can lie **dormant**
for hundreds of years
between eruptions.

The shape and texture of
volcanic rock depends
on how thick the lava
was and how quickly it
cooled and hardened.

MOUNTAINS AND VOLCANOES—FIGURED OUT!

The Andes Mountains in South America stretch for more than 4,350 miles (7,000 kilometers) from north to south, with an average height of 13,000 feet (3,960 m). However, beneath the oceans is a much longer chain, the mid-ocean ridge. It is more than

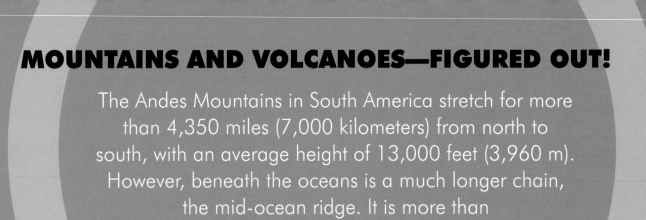

40,000

miles (64,370 km) long.

On average, tectonic plates move at about

1 to 4 inches (2.5 to 10 centimeters) per year. That's about as fast as your fingernails grow!

Some mountains are growing taller in zones where tectonic plates are still pushing together. For example, the Himalayas grow by about

2.4 inches
(6 cm) per year.

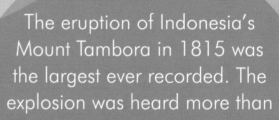

The eruption of Indonesia's Mount Tambora in 1815 was the largest ever recorded. The explosion was heard more than

1,200

miles (1,931 km) away, and at least 71,000 people were killed.

When lava first spews from a volcano, it can be as hot as 1,300 to 2,200 degrees Fahrenheit (702 to 1,204 degrees Celsius). It can flow across the land at speeds of up to

40 miles (64 km) per hour!

Oceans

Oceans cover more than two-thirds of Earth's surface, but we have only explored a small part of their area. They are home to many different animals, and even plants as well. The waters of the oceans are constantly moving, and they help keep Earth's climate stable.

The deeper into the oceans you go, the darker it gets. The pressure also increases deep down because of the enormous weight of the water above pressing down. Because of this, few animals can live in the deepest parts of the ocean.

The top layer of the ocean is called the sunlight zone, and it goes down to about 660 feet (200 m). Here is where most ocean life is found. Beneath it is the twilight zone. Here there is still some faint sunlight, but not enough for plants to grow. Below that is the midnight zone and then the abyssal zone, where it is always dark and few animals are able to survive.

EARTH FIGURED OUT

The ocean floor looks a little like land on the surface, with deep canyons and tall mountains. Much of the ocean floor is covered with muddy **sediments**, made from the remains of plants and animals as well as ash and worn-down rocks.

The warm temperatures and light of the sunlight zone make a great habitat for corals, fish, and other plants and animals.

In some places on the ocean floor, hydrothermal vents release hot water that has a lot of minerals. The vents are home to some unusual creatures.

Lakes

A lake is an area of water that is surrounded by land. There are millions of lakes on Earth: some are small enough to fit in a backyard, while others are hundreds of miles across. The smallest lakes are often called ponds and the largest are sometimes called seas. Some lakes are shallow enough to walk across, but Lake Baikal in Russia is more than 1 mile (1.6 km) deep in some places!

Many lakes were formed by glaciers that carved out hollows in the land as they moved along. When the glaciers melted, the water filled the hollows to create lakes. Other lakes were formed by the movement of tectonic plates, or when a river changed its course.

The water in most lakes is freshwater, but some contain saltwater. Most saltwater lakes do not have rivers leading out of them. The only way for water to leave the lake is by **evaporation**, which usually leaves salt behind.

EARTH FIGURED OUT

Once a volcano is no longer active, sometimes its **crater** fills with rain or melted snow. Other volcanoes might have their top sections blown off in an eruption. This leaves a hollowed-out area called a caldera, which then fills with water.

Many of the lakes in North America were formed about eighteen thousand years ago, when glaciers last covered the land.

Lake Pinatubo in the Philippines formed in a caldera that was created by a huge eruption in 1991. It is now the country's deepest lake.

BODIES OF WATER—FIGURED OUT!

Lake Baikal's surface area of

12,200

square miles (31,598 square kilometers) is less than half the size of Lake Superior. However, it is four times as deep and holds nearly as much water as all five Great Lakes combined!

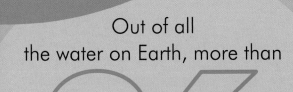

Out of all the water on Earth, more than

96

percent of it is found in the oceans. They contain 321 million cubic miles (1.3 billion cubic km) of water! Only 0.013 percent of Earth's water is found in lakes.

The world's biggest lake by area is the Caspian Sea in Asia, with an area of about

149,000

square miles (385,908 sq km). That's about the same size as Montana!

The tallest volcano on Earth is Ojos del Salado, on the border between Argentina and Chile. In its crater is a small lake, about **33** feet (10 m) deep and 328 feet (100 m) in diameter. It's probably the highest lake in the world.

The Mariana Trench is found in the Pacific Ocean. It is more than **1,580** miles (2,543 km) long and 43 miles (69 km) wide on average. Its deepest point is believed to be 36,070 feet (10,994 m) below the surface.

The temperature at the surface of the oceans can be anywhere between 28 and 97 degrees Fahrenheit (-2 and 36°C). In the midnight zone, the temperature stays steady at about **39°** Fahrenheit (4°C).

Rivers

When water moves across the land in a natural stream, it is called a river. A small river might be just a few miles long, while others flow for thousands of miles. Some only flow for part of the year, when heavy rain or melting snow fills them. Rivers flow downhill, from high ground to lower ground.

Rivers help shape Earth's surface. They can carve out valleys and canyons as they flow over the land, wearing away rocks, soil, and other sediment. They carry that sediment across the land, which creates fertile plains for growing crops. They also form part of the **water cycle**, taking water back to the oceans after it falls as rain.

Humans use rivers, too. We use their water for drinking and washing, and we use boats to transport people and goods for long distances. Rivers are also important habitats for many different plants and animals, from fish to dolphins.

The darker waters of the Rio Negro join the Amazon River as it flows across South America, before entering the Pacific Ocean.

Victoria Falls is located at one of the widest points of the Zambezi River. So much water goes over the falls that it is called "the smoke that thunders."

EARTH FIGURED OUT

When a river's course takes it over a cliff, it can form a spectacular waterfall. Some waterfalls, such as Angel Falls in Venezuela, are incredibly tall. Others, such as Victoria Falls in Africa, are much shorter but very wide.

Canyons

Canyons can be some of Earth's most beautiful landforms. Many of these deep, narrow valleys are formed when a river travels over the land. The enormous weight of a river's water can cut deep into the riverbed. The water carries sediments from the riverbed downstream, making the channel wider.

The steep, rocky sides of canyons are usually caused by **weathering** and **erosion**. When rocks are worn away or broken down, this is called weathering. It can be caused by chemicals in rain that eat away at the rock, or by water getting into cracks in the rocks and then freezing and expanding. This breaks up the rock. When the pieces of rock are washed away, it is called erosion.

Canyons can also be formed by the collision of tectonic plates, which can make part of Earth's crust rise up higher than the land surrounding it. Rivers flowing through this higher land can carve deep canyons.

EARTH FIGURED OUT

A slot canyon is a type of canyon that is much deeper than it is wide. Some of them are only a few feet across at the top! They were formed when fast-flowing water traveled through a narrow crack in the rock.

In this slot canyon, the water has carved the soft rock into beautiful flowing patterns.

The Colorado River cuts through an area of land in Arizona that was pushed up by tectonic plates. Over millions of years, the river carved out deep canyons.

RIVERS—FIGURED OUT!

Many sources say that the Nile River is

4,132

miles (6,650 km) long, and the Amazon River is 3,976 miles (6,399 km) long. However, it is hard to measure the length of a river, and some figures for the Amazon are as high as 4,250 miles (6,840 km). No one can agree whether the Amazon or the Nile is the world's longest river.

Rivers are an important source of freshwater. More than 50 million people live within a few miles of the Nile River, and they depend on its water.

Rivers can be measured by their discharge, which is the total amount of water flowing past a point. The average discharge of the Amazon River is 7,381,000 cubic feet (209,007 cubic meters) per second. The next six rivers on the list, added together, total only 7,243,000 cubic feet (205,099 cu m) per second!

The world's highest waterfall is Angel Falls in Venezuela, which drops a total of 3,212 feet (979 m).

The Grand Canyon is 277 miles (446 km) long, 18 miles (29 km) wide, and 6,000 feet (1,829 m) deep. But it is not the world's longest or deepest canyon. The Yarlung Zangbo Grand Canyon in China is 310 miles (499 km) long and in some places it is more than 17,490 feet (5,331 m) deep.

Islands

An island is a body of land that is completely surrounded by water. **Continents** are also completely surrounded by water, but they are too big to be called islands. The world's largest island, Greenland, covers 836,000 square miles (2,165,230 sq km)—more than three times the size of Texas—but the smallest continent, Australia, is about 3 million square miles (7.8 million sq km).

Islands can be found all over the world, in oceans, lakes, or rivers. They are often found in clusters called archipelagoes. Some islands are tiny with no people living there, and others are home to millions of people.

Some islands were once joined to a continent but were separated when tectonic plates shifted. Others formed when sea levels rose, filling in lower land that joined them to the mainland. Barrier islands form along coastlines, when sand and other sediments pile up. They help protect the coast from storms. Some islands far out in the oceans are the tops of volcanoes rising from the ocean floor.

EARTH FIGURED OUT

People can create islands, too. They make them when they drain wet land or bring in sand or other material from elsewhere.

Artificial islands have been created for hundreds of years. Many were built to make more space for people to live or grow crops.

The Palm Jumeirah in Dubai is an artificial island that was created to look like a palm tree.

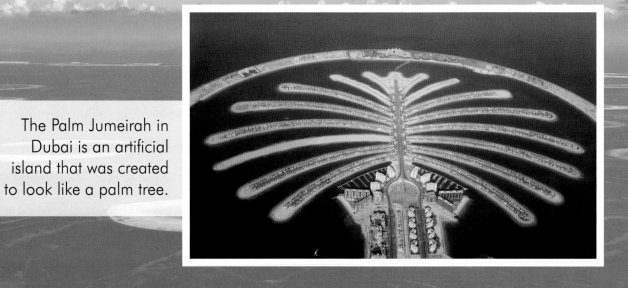

Some islands, such as this one in the Maldives, are formed by living creatures. Corals build up hard outer skeletons, which can break the surface of the water to form islands.

Caves

Some of Earth's most amazing landforms are beneath the surface. A cave is a natural opening in the ground that is large enough for a person to enter it. Some caves are small, single chambers, and others are long, narrow, twisting passages. Some caves have enormous underground chambers.

Caves can form in different types of rock. Many are found in a type of landscape called karst. This is a mixture of rocks including limestone, which can be dissolved by water containing a small amount of acid. Rainwater is slightly acidic, and when it seeps through the soil it becomes more acidic. Over thousands of years, it can wear away large areas of rock.

Some caves have amazing rock formations. Stalactites are like icicles made of rock that hang from the ceiling of a cave. Stalagmites grow up from the floor. Both of these features are formed from minerals in the water that slowly drips from the cave roof.

Some caves are absolutely enormous. The "Big Room" at Carlsbad Caverns in New Mexico is 1,800 feet (549 m) long, with a ceiling 225 feet (69 m) high.

Inside a cave it is usually dark and wet. Many of the animals that live in caves have special **adaptations** for living there. Some are blind, but they have developed other senses that help them. For example, one type of cave fish can find food by feeling vibrations in the water.

Stalagmites often form from water that drips down a stalactite and falls to the floor.

A Home for All

Our planet is more than just a collection of landforms. Earth is also home to a lot of different landscapes, from deserts and polar ice caps to rain forests and prairies. Each landscape is part of a different **ecosystem**, where many different plants and animals find a home.

Animals and plants live together in ecosystems. An ecosystem can be small, such as a pond, or much bigger, such as a forest. The animals and plants that live there depend on each other. For example, plants in a meadow ecosystem might provide food and homes for caterpillars, beetles, and grasshoppers. These insects are eaten by birds, which might be eaten by larger birds or other animals.

All ecosystems are different, and plants and animals have adaptations to survive the conditions where they live. For example, some fish that live in the deepest, darkest parts of the oceans are able to make light with their bodies. This helps them attract prey.

EARTH FIGURED OUT

Animals and plants in deserts have adaptations that help them survive in a hot, dry climate. Kangaroo rats dig burrows where they can stay cool, and they don't need to drink at all—they can get all the moisture they need from the seeds they eat!

A grassland like
this one in Africa can
be home to many
different species of
plants and animals.

Rain forests are one of the
richest habitats on Earth, so it
is important to protect them.

Glossary

adaptations The changes in an organism, over time, that helps it survive and reproduce in a particular habitat.

canyons Narrow valleys with steep sides, often with a stream or river flowing through them.

cliffs Very steep vertical faces of rock or ice.

continents Earth's seven major landmasses.

crater The bowl-shaped hollow around the opening of a volcano.

crust The hard, rocky outer layer of Earth.

deserts Very dry, sandy, or rocky areas with very few plants growing in them.

dormant Not currently active. Many volcanoes can lie dormant for hundreds of years before erupting.

ecosystem A community of living things, together with their environment.

erosion The process by which loosened material is worn away from rocks.

erupt To send out rocks, ash, lava, and gas in a sudden explosion

evaporation The process of turning a liquid into a gas.

fertile Able to support the growth of plants.

fjords Narrow inlets of the sea, found between cliffs or steep slopes.

glaciers Large masses of ice that move very slowly down a slope or across land.

habitats The natural environments of animals or plants.

lava Molten rock that comes out of a volcano.

magma Molten rock beneath Earth's surface.

molten Turned into liquid because of high temperatures.

prairies Large, flat areas of land covered mainly in grasses.

rain forests Dense woodlands with very high rainfall each year, often with trees forming a canopy.

sediments Tiny pieces of rock, soil, and other materials that are carried by flowing water.

tectonic plates Large sections of Earth's crust. Tectonic plates are constantly colliding with or moving away from other plates.

volcanoes Mountains with a hole in the tops or sides that can send out rocks, ash, lava, and gas in an eruption.

water cycle The cycle in which Earth's water turns from vapor in the air into rain or other precipitation and falls to the ground, where it is collected and then evaporates again.

weathering The gradual wearing away of rock by chemical, physical, or biological processes.

Further Reading

Books

Fradin, Judith, and Dennis Fradin. *Volcano!: The Icelandic Eruption of 2010 and Other Hot, Smoky, Fierce, and Fiery Mountains*. Washington, DC: National Geographic Children's Books, 2010.

Labrecque, Ellen. *Mountain Tops.* Earth's Last Frontiers. Chicago: Raintree, 2014.

Meachen Rau, Dana. *U.S. Landforms.* True Books. New York: Children's Press, 2012.

Schneider, Herman, and Nina Schneider. *Rocks, Rivers, and the Changing Earth: A First Book About Geology*. Mineola, NY: Dover Publications, 2014.

Van Rose, Susanna. *Earth.* DK Eyewitness Books. New York: DK Children, 2013.

Websites

This Ocean Explorer website has lots of information about studying the oceans, including some amazing photos:
oceanexplorer.noaa.gov

Watch kids exploring a cave at this site:
pbskids.org/dragonflytv/show/caves.html

This website has pages about many different landforms, as well as information and videos about people who explore them:
science.nationalgeographic.com/science/earth/surface-of-the-earth

You can find the answers to all your questions about volcanoes with this useful website page:
volcano.oregonstate.edu/faqs

Index